HUNGRY CAMPERS

COOKING OUTDOORS
FOR 1 TO 100

ZAC WILLIAMS

Gibbs Smith

Second Edition
27 26 25 24 23   5 4 3 2 1

First Gibbs Smith edition published in 2013
Second Gibbs Smith edition published in 2023
Gibbs Smith
P.O. Box 667
Layton, Utah 84041

1.800.835.4993 orders
www.gibbs-smith.com

Designed by Ryan Thomann and Renee Bond
Printed and bound in China

Gibbs Smith books are printed on paper produced from sustainable PEFC-certified
forest/controlled wood source. Learn more at www.pefc.org.

The Library of Congress has cataloged the first edition as follows:

Williams, Zac.
  Hungry campers : cooking outdoors for 1 to 100 / written and photographed by
Zac Williams. — First edition.
     pages cm
  ISBN 978-1-4236-3028-9 (first edition)
1. Outdoor cooking. I. Title.
  TX823.W523 2013
  641.5'78—dc23
                          2012033196

ISBN 978-1-4236-6351-5

CONTENTS

ACKNOWLEDGMENTS

Thank you to the team at Gibbs Smith for making it possible for me to share my words and photographs throughout the years. Special thanks to Michelle Branson for guiding this new edition of *Hungry Campers* to publication. Thanks to Ryan Thomann and Renee Bond for the terrific design of the book. Continued thanks to my wife, Aimee, and our children, Ethan, Rya, and Piper, for putting up with their crazy cooking dad and waiting to taste until after the photo is captured.

INTRODUCTION:
SAVOR SIMPLICITY

Camping provides an opportunity to step out of our day-to-day lives and to experience nature more closely. For me, sleeping out-doors tends to simplify what's most important. Camping takes me back to the basics of comfort. A dry bed, good company, and of course, great food are all that's needed to enjoy the wild. Delicious food is where this cookbook comes in. By focusing on simple, easy-to-prepare meals, I hope to help campers make the most of their time outdoors.

Recipes are arranged in chapters beginning with ideas for meals that are easy to prepare and teach basic cooking skills, and progressing to more advanced preparations for those camp chefs who are looking for inspiration. Special attention is given to making the job of planning dining operations for scout troops, youth groups, and families easier. Along the way, helpful tips are suggested to make your cooking experience even better. For campers looking for remote adventures, an introduction to backpack cooking with recipes and menus is provided in the last chapter.

Hearty eating should be at the center of any great camping adventure. My childhood memories include watching in anticipation as my dad cooked on our old green double-burner Coleman stove. Now I share my kids' excitement as they create their own campfire meals. Outdoor cooking properly done is just one of the many joys experienced by those who trade a roof at home for the starry sky overhead.

CAMPFIRE COOKING BASICS

For those new to camp cooking, a great place to start is with the basics. Cooking over a fire is perfect because all campers can participate in preparing, cooking, and eating! Ideal for overnight camping trips, these basic recipes require minimal equipment to prepare and clean up easily.

OVERNIGHT CAMPING MENU

DINNER	BREAKFAST	LUNCH
ZIP-BAG SALAD	BROWN BAG CAMPFIRE BREAKFAST	CAMPFIRE NACHOS
PIZZA PITA WITH GARLIC BREAD	CINNAMON TWIRLERS	SLICED FRUIT
BAKED CARAMEL APPLE	HOT COCOA	FRUIT PUNCH
SIMPLE S'MORES	ORANGE JUICE	

CONSTRUCTING A COOKING FIRE

Successful campfire cooking starts before you strike a match. It is important to build a proper fire to create an even bed of hot coals quickly. A good fire requires heat, fuel, and oxygen. A log cabin–style fire, where wood is successively stacked in a square much like a pioneer's log cabin, allows for plenty of air circulation as well as an even spacing of fuel. This type of fire also creates a perfect bed of coals. Wood used in a fire should be dry and preferably seasoned, meaning it comes from a dead tree or was cut months earlier. Hardwoods, such as trimmings from fruit trees, make better coals than softwoods like pine and fir. When starting the fire, tinder of crumpled paper, wood shavings, or other loose flammable material should be ignited under the bottom layer of the fire. Many effective commercial fire-starting products are available that allow for a hot ignition. A properly built fire won't require much tending to create a hot, even bed of coals.

TEMPERATURE OF A COOKING FIRE

Old-timers could easily tell the temperature of cooking coals by holding a hand above the fire. While cooking over a fire takes practice, here is a suggested guideline to estimate the temperature of a fire. Most people can hold their hands 3 to 4 inches above the coals of a high-temperature fire, which is above 400°F, for about 2 seconds. On average, a person can hold a hand above medium-hot coals of about 350°F for 4 seconds, while 6 seconds is an indicator of low-heat coals of 300°F or less. The color of the coals is also an indicator of temperature. More orange signals a higher temperature, and more gray-and-white ash indicates a lower temperature. Most foods cooked directly on the coals in foil do well at medium to low heat to prevent charring, while direct grilling for steaks and chops requires higher temperatures.

CAMP CLEANUP

Besides making camping more pleasant, a clean camp is important for health reasons. Wash hands frequently with biodegradable soap. Take care if you are washing with non-drinkable water, such as what you might find in a stream or lake. Never use soap directly in natural waterways. A well-equipped camp kitchen should include an alcohol-based waterless hand sanitizer to be used after washing with water. Allow the hand sanitizer to evaporate before handling food to prevent unpleasant tastes from transferring.

It's also important to establish a dishwashing procedure that sanitizes dishes and utensils. A simple setup uses two portable washbasins. Scrape off all food residue and wash dishes in hot, soapy water in the first washbasin. In the second rinse basin, add 1 ounce (2 tablespoons) of Clorox per 2½ gallons of water to sanitize. Rinse the dishes and dry.

WRAPPING FOODS IN ALUMINUM FOIL

Foods cooked in aluminum foil do best when steam and heat are kept inside the foil packet. A simple, time-tested way to wrap foods in foil is to use butcher wrap. Heavy-duty aluminum foil is less likely to be punctured when placed in a fire and 18-inch-wide foil is easier to wrap.

1. Place the food in the center of a rectangular piece of aluminum foil, shiny side up.
2. Bring the long sides of the foil together into the center and begin folding down, making 4 to 5 folds to seal (top).
3. Fold each of the short side ends over each other 4 to 5 times, meeting the food in the center (bottom).
4. Place the sealed foil packet seam side down on a second sheet of aluminum foil and repeat to create a double layer for an extra-secure wrap.

STADIUM BRAT

SERVES 1

1 bratwurst sausage
½ small onion, sliced
1 teaspoon butter

1 large roll or hot
   dog bun, slit
Deli mustard or other
   condiments

EQUIPMENT
Campfire coals
Heavy-duty
   aluminum foil

1. Place bratwurst, sliced onions, and butter on a sheet of aluminum foil, shiny side facing up. Wrap securely, taking care to fold edges tightly. Place on the coals and cook 15 to 20 minutes, turning frequently.

2. Serve cooked sausage on the bun and smother with cooked onions. Season with deli mustard or other condiments.

BROWN BAG CAMPFIRE BREAKFAST

SERVES 1

3 strips bacon
2 eggs
1/2 cup frozen hash
   brown potatoes,
   thawed

Salt
Ground black pepper
Hot pepper sauce
   (optional)

EQUIPMENT
Campfire coals
Brown paper bag
   (lunch size)
Stick or marshmallow
   roasting fork

1. Place bacon in the bottom of the bag. Crack eggs into the bag over the bacon. Add hash brown potatoes. Season with salt and black pepper to taste.

2. Fold and roll down the top of the bag until about 3 inches above the potatoes. Insert a stick through the folded portion and cook 5 to 6 inches over low coals for about 10 minutes. It helps to prop up the stick with rocks.

3. Carefully tear off the top of the bag to serve. Season with hot pepper sauce, if desired.

SUNNY-SIDE SANDWICH

SERVES 1

2 eggs
2 slices thick Texas
   toast, or bread
   of choice
1 slice cheddar cheese

1 or 2 single-serve
   mayonnaise packets
Salt
Ground black pepper

EQUIPMENT
Campfire coals
2 large waxed paper
   cups filled with water
Barbecue tongs with
   a long handle
Heavy leather gloves
Heavy-duty
   aluminum foil

1. Place each egg into one of the cups filled with water. Using the tongs and gloves, carefully place each cup on the hot coals. Allow the water to boil for 6 minutes, until the eggs are soft-boiled.

2. While eggs are boiling, place the slices of bread on a sheet of aluminum foil, shiny side facing up, and toast at the edge of the fire for 5 minutes.

3. Carefully remove eggs from the fire with the tongs. Crack and serve between the slices of toasted bread with the cheese and mayonnaise. Season with salt and black pepper to taste.

CINNAMON TWIRLERS

SERVES 2 TO 4

1 (12.4-ounce)
  can refrigerated
  cinnamon rolls
  with icing

EQUIPMENT
Campfire coals
$\frac{1}{4}$-inch-thick wooden
  stick or dowel

1. Open the can of cinnamon rolls, separating and unwinding each roll. Wrap each strip of dough around the stick, pressing the ends together.

2. Cook for about 8 minutes, 8 to 10 inches away from the coals, rotating the stick to cook evenly. Drizzle with icing.

BOX TURNOVERS

SERVES 2 TO 4

1 can refrigerated
  biscuits
1 (10.25-ounce) jar
  jam (strawberry,
  raspberry, or peach
  works well)
Decorating sugar

EQUIPMENT
Campfire coals
Open-top cardboard
  box (copy paper size)
Heavy-duty
  aluminum foil

3 rocks or bricks,
  about 5 inches tall
Small baking sheet
  or pie tin
Fire-resistant mitt
  or tongs

1. Cover the box completely on all sides, inside and out, with 2 layers of aluminum foil, shiny side facing out, making sure no cardboard is visible.

2. Open refrigerated biscuits, separating and flattening each one slightly. Spoon the jam into the center of each round of biscuit dough. Fold over and pinch the edges to seal. Sprinkle generously with decorating sugar. Place the turnovers on the baking sheet or in the pie tin.

3. Over low coals (no flames), place 3 rocks or bricks into a tripod shape to support the cookie sheet or pie tin. Lower the cardboard box over turnovers and bake for 8 to 12 minutes, checking every few minutes.

This box oven can also be used to make rolls, biscuits, and mini cupcakes or to cook small pizzas.

ZIP-BAG SALAD

SERVES 1

2 cups iceberg
   lettuce, chopped
2 or 3 cherry tomatoes

2 tablespoons grated
   Parmesan cheese
2 tablespoons prepared
   Italian dressing

EQUIPMENT
1 quart-size resealable
   freezer bag

Combine all ingredients in the resealable bag and shake to coat. Eat out of the bag or empty onto a plate.

CAMPFIRE NACHOS

SERVES 1

2 cups tortilla chips
1/2 (16-ounce) can
   refried beans, stirred
1 cup shredded
   Mexican-style
   cheese blend

1/4 cup sliced bottled
   jalapeño peppers
   (optional)
1/4 cup prepared salsa
1/4 cup sour cream

EQUIPMENT
Campfire coals
10-inch disposable
   aluminum takeout
   dish (available at
   dollar stores)
Heavy-duty
   aluminum foil
3 rocks or bricks,
   about 4 inches
   high, arranged on
   coals like a tripod

1. Spread the tortilla chips in the aluminum takeout dish and top with spoonfuls of refried beans. Cover with cheese. Wrap the entire dish with aluminum foil.

2. Place the wrapped dish on the rock or brick tripod over the coals. Cook for about 10 to 15 minutes, until the beans are hot and the cheese is melted. Serve topped with jalapeños (if using), salsa, and sour cream.

PIZZA PITA WITH GARLIC BREAD

SERVES 1

2 flatbread pita rounds
2 tablespoons pizza
   or marinara sauce
1/4 cup shredded
   mozzarella cheese
Assorted pizza top-
   pings (pepperoni,
   diced ham, mush-
   rooms, canned

pineapple, green
   bell pepper slices,
   sliced black olives)
Italian seasoning
1 loaf French bread
1/2 cup butter
1/2 to 1 teaspoon
   garlic powder

EQUIPMENT
Campfire coals
Heavy-duty
   aluminum foil

1. Place 1 pita round on a sheet of aluminum foil, shiny side facing up. Spread the sauce over the pita and add cheese and toppings as desired. Sprinkle with Italian seasoning to taste.

2. Cover with the remaining pita.

3. Wrap aluminum foil over pitas and fold in edges to seal. Place over coals and cook for 10 to 12 minutes, turning once halfway through.

4. Cut French bread into slices three-quarters of the way through. Stuff each slit with butter and garlic powder. Wrap loaf in aluminum foil and cook over the coals for about 10 to 12 minutes.

CLASSIC TINFOIL DINNER

SERVES 1

1 (⅓-pound) ground
  beef patty, thawed
Ground black pepper
Garlic salt

1 cup cubed potatoes
½ cup baby carrots
½ onion, sliced
2 tablespoons ketchup

EQUIPMENT
Campfire coals
Heavy-duty
  aluminum foil

1. Place the ground beef patty on a sheet of aluminum foil, shiny side facing up, and season with black pepper and garlic salt to taste. Add potatoes, carrots, and onions, and top with ketchup. Fold the long sides of the aluminum foil inward and seal. Roll short ends securely into the middle.

2. Place wrapped dinner on coals and cook for 10 minutes on each side. Open carefully to avoid steam burns, and serve.

In place of ketchup, substitute ½ a can of cream of mushroom soup for a delicious variation.

EASY LEMON BUTTER TROUT

SERVES 1

1 (8- to 12-inch) fresh
   trout, cleaned
   and dressed
2 tablespoons
   butter, softened

1 teaspoon lemon
   pepper
Tartar sauce (optional)

EQUIPMENT
Campfire coals
Heavy-duty
   aluminum foil

1. Place trout on a sheet of aluminum foil, shiny side facing up. Spread the softened butter along the inside of the fish. While holding the fish open, sprinkle the lemon pepper liberally over butter. Wrap fish in foil, sealing edges and ends well. Place the wrapped fish seam side down and repeat the wrap with a second sheet of foil.

2. Place the wrapped fish on coals for 8 to 12 minutes, depending on the size of the trout. When cooked, the meat will pull away from the bones, which can be easily removed and discarded. The skin will slide off. Serve with tartar sauce.

BAKED CARAMEL APPLE

SERVES 1

1 Golden Delicious apple

3 or 4 soft caramel candies
1 tablespoon butter

EQUIPMENT
Campfire coals
Heavy-duty aluminum foil

1. Cut out and remove the top ¾ of the core of the apple, taking care not to cut through the bottom. Place the caramel candies into the hollowed-out apple and top with butter.

2. Wrap apple in aluminum foil and place right side up on coals. Cook for 12 to 14 minutes, until apple is soft and candies have melted. If necessary, give the butter and caramel a stir to combine.

BANANA BOAT

SERVES 1

1 banana
1/4 cup chocolate chips

Mini marshmallows

EQUIPMENT
Campfire coals
Heavy-duty
aluminum foil

1. Cut a 1-inch-wide flap down the length of the banana peel, leaving the peel attached at the bottom. Open the flap and cut a row of notches out of the banana, leaving space between each banana square. Eat or discard these extra banana pieces.

2. Stuff each space with chocolate chips and a mini marshmallow. Replace flap of banana and wrap the banana in aluminum foil, shiny side facing up. Place on coals, leaving the stem side up, and cook for 8 to 10 minutes. Unwrap and serve.

SIMPLE S'MORES

MAKES AS MANY AS YOU WANT

1 bag large
   marshmallows

1 package fudge-
   covered graham
   cracker cookies

EQUIPMENT
Campfire coals
Cooking sticks

Roast a marshmallow on a stick over a fire, turning frequently. When the marshmallow is hot and toasty, slide it onto a fudge graham cookie and top with another cookie. Eat quickly!

VARIATIONS: For s'more fun, try different types of cookies, including cinnamon grahams, fudge-covered mint cookies, or gingersnaps. To add flavoring to your marshmallows, try cutting a small slit and inserting mini peanut butter cups, Rolos, M&Ms, cut-up Snickers bars, or other candies. You can also squeeze in a shot of flavored Italian syrups using a small kitchen squeeze bottle for an added burst of strawberry, vanilla, orange, or any other flavor.

LARGE GROUP COOKING

Memories are made in the outdoors when people come together to share the experience. For family reunions, youth groups and troops, and community meet-ups, this also means feeding a lot of hungry campers as deliciously and easily as possible.

Camp stoves running on propane are best for large-scale kitchen operations. These recipes are designed to scale up from 12 to 100 or even more to fit your group size. Keep in mind you might need to cook in batches and plan on additional equipment and cooks.

SUMMER CAMP MENU

DAY 1

LUNCH
SUB SANDWICHES

POTATO CHIPS

DINNER
ZIP-BAG SALAD

IRISH SPAGHETTI

PUMPERNICKEL BREAD

SIMPLE S'MORES

DAY 2

BREAKFAST
MÜESLI

LUNCH
GRILLED ONION
PEPPER DOGS

MULTI-GRAIN CHIPS

DINNER
CHICKEN AND
DUMPLINGS

NO-FRIDGE FRUIT
SALAD

SODA POP COBBLER

DAY 3

BREAKFAST
IRISH BREAKFAST

LUNCH
CHEESE 'N' MAC

CRACKERS

SLICED FRESH
VEGETABLES

DINNER
REALLY SLOPPY JOES

EASY SLAW

BAKED CARAMEL
APPLES

DAY 4

BREAKFAST
FRENCH TOAST
CASSEROLE

LUNCH
CAMPFIRE NACHOS

GREEN SALAD

DINNER
TACORITTOS

SCONES

DAY 5

BREAKFAST
PUMPKIN SPICE
PANCAKES

LUNCH
PEANUT BUTTER
SANDWICH BAR

VEGETABLE CHIPS

DINNER
BEEF GOULASH

FRENCH BREAD

CINNAMON TWIRLERS

BANANA BOAT

DAY 6

BREAKFAST
FOREST HOT CEREAL

CAMP COOKING DUTIES

While youth groups understand the importance of an assignment roster on a camping trip to distribute camp cooking responsibilities equally, having either a formal or informal system of dividing responsibilities can also be helpful for families and groups of friends. Equally dividing kitchen jobs not only ensures that one person isn't overly burdened, but it also gives everyone an opportunity to experience the fun of cooking outdoors. While organized groups may find it necessary to maintain a schedule that allows for an equal rotation, less formal methods may include assigning a member of the party to make sure tasks are divided evenly.

CHOOSING AN EXPEDITION STOVE

Efficient cooking for more than two people requires a larger expedition camp stove with two or more burners. The most common types of stoves are fueled by propane or liquid white gas. A propane camp stove is the most similar to a standard natural gas home range and has the advantage of being easy to operate. Simply turn the burner knob and light. Propane stoves also can offer more room for cooking through extra burners, and are often self-supported at waist level. Many manufacturers make integrated griddles or even smoke boxes for grilling burgers and meat. Propane stoves have the disadvantage of usually being larger and heavier than white gas stoves. Many also require full-size LP tanks similar to a gas grill, which take up space and can be heavy.

White gas camp stoves tend to be smaller and lighter, which is nice if you have limited packing space. Liquid fuels are also easy to refuel while camping, which can be a benefit. While both types of stoves perform more poorly at altitude and low temperatures, white gas generally produces more heat than comparable propane stoves in adverse conditions. Liquid fuel stoves tend to be more difficult to operate. It's important to learn how to use the stove before the trip begins.

CAMP KITCHEN ESSENTIAL TOOLS

While camping requires a certain amount of learning how to make do without conveniences found in a home kitchen, taking time to assemble a few essential tools can make life a lot easier in the field. An easy way to keep implements accessible is to store them in a fabric shoe hanger or a specialized camp-cooking organizer. Roll up the storage hanger and place it in a plastic storage bin with pots, pans, and other gear. This list may be helpful for stocking your camp kitchen:

Chef's knife

Small knife

Plastic cutting board

Pancake turner

Wire whisk

Large serving and
   mixing spoon

Ladle

Large mixing bowl

Small mixing bowl

Can opener

Vegetable peeler

Measuring spoons

Measuring cups

Wash basins (2)

Biodegradable
   dish soap

Small bottle of
   liquid bleach
   (for sanitizing)

GIANT "OMELETS"

12 SERVINGS

1 stick butter
3 dozen eggs, beaten
3/4 cup milk
1/2 teaspoon ground
   black pepper
3/4 teaspoon salt
1 pound chopped ham
1 onion, diced
2 green bell
   peppers, diced
1 pound shredded
   cheddar Jack cheese

25 SERVINGS

2 sticks butter
6 dozen eggs, beaten
1 1/2 cups milk
1 teaspoon ground
   black pepper
1 1/2 teaspoons salt
2 pounds chopped ham
2 onions, diced
4 green bell
   peppers, diced
2 pounds shredded
   cheddar Jack cheese

50 SERVINGS

4 sticks butter
12 dozen eggs, beaten
3 cups milk
2 teaspoons ground
   black pepper
1 tablespoon salt
4 pounds chopped ham
4 onions, diced
8 green bell
   peppers, diced
4 pounds shredded
   cheddar Jack cheese

EQUIPMENT
Camp stove
Large griddle

1. Preheat the griddle over medium heat, melting the butter. Combine milk with beaten eggs and mix well. Add black pepper and salt.

2. Add ham, onions, and bell peppers to the hot griddle, cooking for 3 to 5 minutes, until onions are translucent. Pour egg mixture over the ham mixture and let cook for 3 to 4 minutes, until set. Cut into sections and turn over as needed to cook the other side. A large recipe may need to be cooked in batches.

3. In the last few minutes, top with shredded cheese, cooking to melt.

IRISH BREAKFAST

12 SERVINGS

1 pound bacon
2 pounds link sausage
6 cups fresh sliced mushrooms
1 (32-ounce) package frozen hash browns, southern-style or cube, thawed
2 dozen eggs, beaten
3 small tomatoes, sliced
½ teaspoon ground black pepper
1 teaspoon salt
Chopped parsley

25 SERVINGS

2 pound bacon
4 pounds link sausage
2 pounds fresh sliced mushrooms
2 (32-ounce) packages frozen hash browns, southern-style or cube, thawed
4 dozen eggs, beaten
6 tomatoes, sliced
1 teaspoon ground black pepper
2 teaspoons salt
Chopped parsley

50 SERVINGS

4 pounds bacon
8 pounds link sausage
4 pounds fresh sliced mushrooms
2 (64-ounce) packages frozen hash browns, southern-style or cube, thawed
8 dozen eggs, beaten
12 tomatoes, sliced
2 teaspoons ground black pepper
4 teaspoons salt
Chopped parsley

EQUIPMENT
Camp stove
Large griddle

1. Cook bacon and sausage together on griddle until done, then cut into bite-size pieces. Set aside and drain off most of the grease. Cook sliced mushrooms until soft and set aside.

2. Add frozen hash browns and cook, turning frequently, until browned.

3. Return the sausage, bacon, and the sautéed mushrooms to the griddle with the hash browns. Push the mixture to the side, making room

to pour the eggs onto the griddle. Gently fold the eggs over as they cook instead of chopping. As the eggs start to set, begin mixing them into the hash brown mixture.

4. Add the sliced tomatoes, cooking briefly until warmed. Season with black pepper and salt. Garnish with parsley.

STOVETOP SODA BREAD

12 SERVINGS
6 cups all-purpose
   flour
1½ teaspoons salt
1 tablespoon
   baking soda
3 cups buttermilk or
   ¾ cup buttermilk
   powder and
   3 cups water

25 SERVINGS
12 cups all-
   purpose flour
1 tablespoon salt
3 tablespoons
   baking soda
1½ quarts buttermilk
   or 1½ cups
   buttermilk powder
   and 1½ quarts water

50 SERVINGS
6 pounds plus 2 cups
   all-purpose flour
2 tablespoons salt
⅓ cup baking soda
3 quarts buttermilk or
   3 cups buttermilk
   powder and 3 quarts
   water

EQUIPMENT
Camp stove
Large, deep, heavy skillet (large recipe may require several skillets)

1. Mix dry ingredients together well in a bowl and add the buttermilk. Knead lightly with floured hands. Preheat a heavy skillet on the stove over medium heat.

2. Form the dough into a flat circle the size of the skillet, about ½ inch thick. Sprinkle flour into the preheated skillet and add the dough. Quickly score the top of the dough into 4 quarters with a knife.

3. Cook the bread for 6 to 8 minutes per side until golden brown, and serve with butter, jam, and honey. For large quantities, rounds of dough can be cooked on a griddle.

FRENCH TOAST CASSEROLE

12 SERVINGS
1 stick butter
2 dozen eggs, beaten
1 pint half-and-half
3/4 tablespoon
   vanilla extract
6 tablespoons sugar
12 slices cooked
   bacon, crumbled
24 slices hearty bread,
   cut into 1-inch
   sections lengthwise
Powdered sugar
Maple syrup

25 SERVINGS
2 sticks butter
4 dozen eggs, beaten
1 quart half-and-half
1 1/2 tablespoons
   vanilla extract
3/4 cup sugar
1 pound cooked
   bacon, crumbled
3 loaves hearty sliced
   bread, cut into 1-inch
   sections lengthwise
Powdered sugar
Maple syrup

50 SERVINGS
4 sticks butter
8 dozen eggs, beaten
2 quarts half-and-half
3 tablespoons
   vanilla extract
1 1/2 cups sugar
2 pounds cooked
   bacon, crumbled
6 loaves hearty sliced
   bread, cut into 1-inch
   sections lengthwise
Powdered sugar
Maple syrup

EQUIPMENT
Camp stove
Large, deep, heavy skillet (large recipe may require several skillets)

1. In a large skillet over medium heat, melt the butter. Mix together eggs, half-and-half, vanilla, sugar, and crumbled bacon, beating until well blended. Place bread strips in skillet and pour egg mixture over top.

2. Cook over medium heat for 8 to 10 minutes, until bottom browns and eggs begin to set. Flip over in sections and cook for another 4 to 5 minutes. Serve with powdered sugar and maple syrup.

PUMPKIN SPICED PANCAKES

12 SERVINGS

1 (29-ounce) can
   pumpkin
6 cups pancake mix
4 cups cold water
3 teaspoons pumpkin
   pie spice
Maple syrup

25 SERVINGS

2 (29-ounce) cans
   pumpkin
12 cups pancake mix
2 quarts cold water
2 tablespoons
   pumpkin pie spice
Maple syrup

50 SERVINGS

4 (29-ounce) cans
   pumpkin
6 pounds plus 2 cups
   pancake mix
1 gallon cold water
4 tablespoons
   pumpkin pie spice
Maple syrup

EQUIPMENT

Camp stove
Large griddle

1. Combine all ingredients together except syrup and mix briefly until blended.

2. Pour 5-inch pancakes onto a lightly greased griddle over medium-high heat and cook until batter starts to bubble; flip and cook on other side. Serve with syrup.

MÜESLI

12 SERVINGS
6 cups rolled oats
2 (32-ounce)
  containers
  vanilla yogurt
3 cups blueberries
2 pints strawberries,
  sliced
6 bananas, sliced
3 apples, diced
3/4 cup chopped
  candied walnuts
  (optional)

25 SERVINGS
2 1/2 pounds rolled oats
4 (32-ounce)
  containers
  vanilla yogurt
2 pints blueberries
4 pints strawberries,
  sliced
4 pounds bananas,
  sliced
6 apples, diced
1 1/2 cups chopped
  candied walnuts
  (optional)

50 SERVINGS
5 pounds rolled oats
8 (32-ounce)
  containers
  vanilla yogurt
4 pints blueberries
8 pints strawberries,
  sliced
8 pounds bananas,
  sliced
12 apples, diced
3 cups chopped
  candied walnuts
  (optional)

EQUIPMENT
Large mixing bowl

In a large mixing bowl, combine all ingredients, stirring gently to coat. Serve topped with chopped candied walnuts, if desired.

FOREST HOT CEREAL

12 SERVINGS

1½ quarts water
¾ teaspoon salt
4 cups steel-cut
  or Irish oats
1½ cups brown sugar
3 Granny Smith
  apples, diced
1½ cups golden raisins
3 teaspoons cinnamon
Half-and-half

25 SERVINGS

3 quarts water
1½ teaspoons salt
8 cups steel-cut
  or Irish oats
3 cups brown sugar
6 Granny Smith
  apples, diced
3 cups golden raisins
1 tablespoon cinnamon
Half-and-half

50 SERVINGS

6 quarts water
  (1½ gallons)
1 tablespoon salt
16 cups steel-cut
  or Irish oats
2⅔ pounds
  brown sugar
12 Granny Smith
  apples, diced
6 cups golden raisins
2 tablespoons
  cinnamon
Half-and-half

EQUIPMENT
Camp stove
Large pot

Bring water to a boil over high heat and add salt. Add oats and cook for about 10 minutes. Cover the pot and let stand for an additional 5 minutes. Mix in brown sugar, diced apples, golden raisins, and cinnamon. Serve topped with half-and-half.

SUB SANDWICHES

12 SERVINGS

12 large sub rolls,
   sliced
1 (15-ounce) jar relish
   sandwich spread
3 pounds assorted
   sliced cold cuts
24 ounces
   (1½ pounds) sliced
   provolone cheese
6 cups shredded
   iceberg lettuce
6 tomatoes, sliced
Salt
Ground black pepper

25 SERVINGS

25 large sub rolls,
   sliced
2 (15-ounce) jars relish
   sandwich spread
6 pounds assorted
   sliced cold cuts
3 pounds sliced
   provolone cheese
12 cups shredded
   iceberg lettuce
12 tomatoes, sliced
Salt
Ground black pepper

50 SERVINGS

50 large sub rolls,
   sliced
4 (15-ounce) jars relish
   sandwich spread
12 pounds assorted
   sliced cold cuts
6 pounds sliced
   provolone cheese
24 cups shredded
   iceberg lettuce
24 tomatoes, sliced
Salt
Ground black pepper

Assemble sub sandwiches by first spreading both sides of each roll with sandwich spread and then stacking with meat, cheese, lettuce, and tomatoes. Sprinkle with salt and black pepper to taste.

PEANUT BUTTER SANDWICH BAR

12 SERVINGS

3 loaves white bread
1 (40-ounce) jar
  peanut butter
2 (7-ounce)
  jars whipped
  marshmallow cream
1 (26.5-ounce)
  jar Nutella
1 (32-ounce) jar
  grape jelly
6 sliced bananas
2 thinly sliced apples
2 cups shredded
  coconut
2 cups chopped
  peanuts

25 SERVINGS

6 loaves white bread
2 (40-ounce) jars
  peanut butter
4 (7-ounce)
  jars whipped
  marshmallow cream
2 (26.5-ounce)
  jars Nutella
2 (32-ounce) jars
  grape jelly
4 pounds sliced
  bananas
4 thinly sliced apples
4 cups shredded
  coconut
4 cups chopped
  peanuts

50 SERVINGS

12 loaves white bread
4 (40-ounce) jars
  peanut butter
6 (7-ounce)
  jars whipped
  marshmallow cream
4 (26.5-ounce)
  jars Nutella
4 (32-ounce) jars
  grape jelly
8 pounds sliced
  bananas
8 thinly sliced apples
8 cups shredded
  coconut
8 cups chopped
  peanuts

Spread out ingredients on a table and let each guest build their perfect peanut butter sandwich.

REALLY SLOPPY JOES

12 SERVINGS

3 pounds lean ground beef, crumbled

2 teaspoons ground black pepper

2 tablespoons garlic salt

2 onions, diced

2 green bell peppers, diced

3 (10.75-ounce) cans condensed chicken gumbo soup

1/4 cup barbecue sauce

3 3/4 cups water

12 large seeded hamburger buns

Dill pickle slices

25 SERVINGS

6 pounds lean ground beef, crumbled

4 teaspoons ground black pepper

4 tablespoons garlic salt

4 onions, diced

4 green bell peppers, diced

6 (10.75-ounce) cans condensed chicken gumbo soup

1/2 cup barbecue sauce

7 1/2 cups water

25 large seeded hamburger buns

Dill pickle slices

50 SERVINGS

12 pounds lean ground beef, crumbled

3 tablespoons ground black pepper

1/2 cup garlic salt

8 onions, diced

8 green bell peppers, diced

12 (10.75-ounce) cans condensed chicken gumbo soup

1 cup barbecue sauce

3 3/4 quarts water

50 large seeded hamburger buns

Dill pickle slices

EQUIPMENT

Camp stove

Large, deep, heavy skillet (large recipe may require two skillets)

1. Brown the ground beef in the skillet over medium-high heat, adding black pepper and garlic salt. Add onions and bell peppers, cooking until soft. Drain off any excess fat.

2. Stir in the chicken gumbo soup, barbecue sauce, and water, continuing to simmer over low heat for about 10 minutes. Serve on buns with dill pickle slices.

CHEESEBURGER STEW

12 SERVINGS
3 pounds lean ground beef, crumbled

3 teaspoons salt

1½ teaspoons ground black pepper

3 onions, chopped

3 (26-ounce) cans tomato soup

3 quarts water

3 cups dried macaroni

2 (15-ounce) jars Cheez Whiz

25 SERVINGS
6 pounds lean ground beef, crumbled

2 tablespoons salt

1 tablespoon ground black pepper

6 onions, chopped

6 (26-ounce) cans tomato soup

1½ gallons water

6 cups dried macaroni

4 (15-ounce) jars Cheez Whiz

50 SERVINGS
12 pounds lean ground beef, crumbled

4 tablespoons salt

2 tablespoons ground black pepper

12 onions, chopped

7 (50-ounce) cans tomato soup

3 gallons water

12 cups dried macaroni

1 (#10) can Cheez Whiz

EQUIPMENT
Camp stove
Large heavy pot

1. In the bottom of a large heavy pot, brown ground beef over medium-high heat, seasoning with salt and black pepper. When the meat is almost brown, add chopped onions, continuing to cook for 3 to 4 more minutes until translucent. Drain off any excess fat.

2. Add tomato soup, water, and dried macaroni. Continue cooking for 10 to 14 more minutes, until the macaroni is soft. Stir in Cheez Whiz and serve with sliced French bread.

GRILLED ONION PEPPER DOGS

12 SERVINGS
24 beef hot dogs
   (3 pounds)
1/4 cup butter
3 onions, sliced
3 cups pickled sliced
   banana peppers
24 hot dog buns
Mustard
Ketchup

25 SERVINGS
6 pounds beef hot dogs
1 stick butter
6 onions, sliced
6 cups pickled sliced
   banana peppers
50 hot dog buns
Mustard
Ketchup

50 SERVINGS
12 pounds beef
   hot dogs
2 sticks butter
12 onions, sliced
1 (96-ounce) jar
   pickled sliced
   banana peppers
100 hot dog buns
Mustard
Ketchup

EQUIPMENT
Camp stove
Large griddle

1. Heat the griddle over medium-high heat. Slice each hot dog lengthwise down the middle and grill on the griddle for 5 to 7 minutes, turning frequently until browned. Add butter, onions, and banana peppers, and cook until the onions are soft and translucent, stirring frequently.

2. Serve the hot dogs on buns smothered with onions and peppers. Add mustard and ketchup as desired.

IRISH SPAGHETTI

12 SERVINGS

- 3 pounds uncooked spaghetti noodles
- 3 pounds lean ground beef, crumbled
- 1½ teaspoons ground black pepper
- 2 tablespoons garlic salt
- 2 onions, diced
- 3 (10.75-ounce) cans condensed tomato soup
- 3 (10.75-ounce) cans condensed cream of mushroom soup
- 1½ cups water
- 3 tablespoons Italian seasoning

25 SERVINGS

- 6 pounds uncooked spaghetti noodles
- 6 pounds lean ground beef, crumbled
- 1 tablespoon ground black pepper
- 4 tablespoons garlic salt
- 4 onions, diced
- 6 (10.75-ounce) cans condensed tomato soup
- 6 (10.75-ounce) cans condensed cream of mushroom soup
- 3 cups water
- ⅓ cup Italian seasoning

50 SERVINGS

- 12 pounds uncooked spaghetti noodles
- 12 pounds lean ground beef, crumbled
- 2 tablespoons ground black pepper
- ½ cup garlic salt
- 8 onions, diced
- 5 (26-ounce) family-size cans condensed tomato soup
- 5 (26-ounce) family-size cans condensed cream of mushroom soup
- 6 cups water
- ⅔ cup Italian seasoning

EQUIPMENT

Camp stove

Large pot

Large, deep, heavy skillet (large recipe may require 2 skillets)

1. Prepare spaghetti noodles according to package instructions.

2. Brown ground beef in the skillet over medium-high heat, adding black pepper and garlic salt. Add the onions, cooking until soft and translucent. Drain off any excess fat. Stir in the soups, water, and Italian seasoning. Bring to a simmer over low heat and cook for 10 minutes. Serve over hot spaghetti noodles.

TACORITTOS

12 SERVINGS

3 pounds lean ground beef, crumbled

3 packages taco seasoning

3 (15-ounce) cans pinto beans, undrained

3 (10-ounce) cans Rotel diced tomatoes and green chiles, undrained

24 ounces shredded Mexican-style cheese

1 regular bag nacho cheese Doritos

6 cups shredded iceberg lettuce

16 ounces sour cream

25 SERVINGS

6 pounds lean ground beef, crumbled

1 cup taco seasoning

1 (#10) can pinto beans, undrained

6 (10-ounce) cans Rotel diced tomatoes and green chiles, undrained

3 pounds shredded Mexican-style cheese

2 regular bags nacho cheese Doritos

12 cups shredded iceberg lettuce

32 ounces sour cream

50 SERVINGS

12 pounds lean ground beef, crumbled

2 cups taco seasoning

2 (#10) cans pinto beans, undrained

12 (10-ounce) cans Rotel diced tomatoes and green chiles, undrained

6 pounds shredded Mexican-style cheese

4 regular bags nacho cheese Doritos

24 cups shredded iceberg lettuce

64 ounces sour cream

EQUIPMENT

Camp stove

Large, deep, heavy skillet (large recipe may require 2 skillets)

1. Brown ground beef in the skillet over medium-high heat. Drain off any excess fat. Add taco seasoning, pinto beans, and tomatoes and green chiles. Continue simmering for 8 to 10 minutes to reduce liquid.

2. Stir in shredded cheese and Doritos until cheese is melted. Serve topped with shredded lettuce and sour cream.

VARIATION: For a Navajo taco, make the recipe without adding Doritos and serve over scones with lettuce, salsa, and sour cream.

BEEF GOULASH

12 SERVINGS

2 1/2 pounds uncooked spiral pasta
3 tablespoons vegetable oil
2 pounds flank steak, cut into strips
2 teaspoons salt
3 teaspoons ground black pepper
3 teaspoons garlic powder
2 large onions, chopped
2 red bell peppers, chopped
1/3 cup all-purpose flour
3 (14.5-ounce) cans diced tomatoes, undrained
3 (14-ounce) cans beef broth
3 teaspoons paprika

25 SERVINGS

5 pounds uncooked spiral pasta
1/3 cup vegetable oil
6 pounds flank steak, cut into strips
1 1/2 tablespoons salt
2 tablespoons ground black pepper
2 tablespoons garlic powder
4 large onions, chopped
4 red bell peppers, chopped
1 cup all-purpose flour
6 (14.5-ounce) cans diced tomatoes, undrained
3 (32-ounce) cartons beef broth
2 tablespoons paprika

50 SERVINGS

10 pounds uncooked spiral pasta
2/3 cup vegetable oil
12 pounds flank steak, cut into strips
3 tablespoons salt
4 tablespoons ground black pepper
4 tablespoons garlic powder
8 large onions, chopped
8 red bell peppers, chopped
2 cups all-purpose flour
12 (14.5-ounce) cans diced tomatoes, undrained
6 (32-ounce) cartons beef broth
4 tablespoons paprika

EQUIPMENT

Camp stove
Large, deep, heavy skillet or Dutch oven (large recipe may require 2 skillets)

1. Prepare pasta according to package directions. In a large skillet, heat oil over medium-high heat, then add steak strips, salt, black pepper, and

garlic powder. Cook for 5 to 6 minutes until browned. Add onions and red bell peppers, and continue to cook until slightly softened.

2. Add flour to oil and drippings in the skillet and stir until a smooth paste is formed. Add remaining ingredients and continue simmering over low heat for 8 to 10 more minutes. Serve over drained pasta.

CHEESE 'N' MAC

12 SERVINGS

48 ounces (3 pounds) uncooked large elbow macaroni

1 1/2 cups butter

1 (28-ounce) can petite-diced tomatoes, undrained

24 ounces (1 1/2 pounds) shredded Mexican-style cheese blend

3/4 teaspoon ground black pepper

Salt

25 SERVINGS

6 pounds uncooked large elbow macaroni

6 sticks butter

2 (28-ounce) cans petite-diced tomatoes, undrained

3 pounds shredded Mexican-style cheese blend

1 1/2 teaspoons ground black pepper

Salt

50 SERVINGS

12 pounds uncooked large elbow macaroni

12 sticks butter

4 (28-ounce) cans petite-diced tomatoes, undrained

6 pounds shredded Mexican-style cheese blend

3 teaspoons ground black pepper

Salt

EQUIPMENT

Camp stove

Large heavy pot

In a large pot, cover the macaroni with at least 3 inches of water, boil until tender, and then drain. Keeping the macaroni hot in the pot over low heat, add butter, tomatoes, shredded cheese, black pepper, and salt. Serve immediately.

CHICKEN AND DUMPLINGS

12 SERVINGS

3 cups biscuit mix
  (Bisquick)
1 cup milk
3 tablespoons olive
  or vegetable oil
1 pound baby carrots
12 boneless skinless
  chicken breasts
  (4 pounds)
3 (10.75-ounce) cans
  condensed cream
  of chicken soup
3 (10.75-ounce) cans
  condensed golden
  mushroom soup
1½ cups water
3 (4-ounce) cans
  mushrooms, drained

25 SERVINGS

6 cups biscuit mix
  (Bisquick)
2 cups milk
⅓ cup olive or
  vegetable oil
2 pounds baby carrots
25 boneless skinless
  chicken breasts
  (8 pounds)
3 (26-ounce)
  family-size cans
  condensed cream
  of chicken soup
5 (10.75-ounce) cans
  condensed golden
  mushroom soup
3 cups water
6 (4-ounce) cans
  mushrooms, drained

50 SERVINGS

12 cups biscuit mix
  (Bisquick)
1 quart milk
⅔ cup olive or
  vegetable oil
4 pounds baby carrots
50 boneless skinless
  chicken breasts
  (16 pounds)
2 (50-ounce) cans
  condensed cream
  of chicken soup
12 (10.75-ounce) cans
  condensed golden
  mushroom soup
1½ quarts water
1 (#10) can mushrooms,
  drained

EQUIPMENT

Camp stove
Large, deep, heavy-lidded skillet or Dutch oven (large recipe
  may require several large skillets or roasting pans)

1. Combine biscuit mix and milk to form a soft dough and set aside.

2. In a heavy skillet, heat the oil over medium-high heat. Add carrots and chicken breasts and cook for 6 minutes, turning often to brown. Add soups, water, and mushrooms, bringing the mixture to a simmer. Drop large spoonfuls of dough onto the chicken and vegetables to form dumplings. Cover and cook for 15 to 20 more minutes, until dumplings are done.

NO-FRIDGE FRUIT SALAD

12 SERVINGS

1 (20-ounce) can crushed pineapple

4 (15-ounce) cans mandarin oranges, undrained

2 large boxes instant lemon pudding

2 (29-ounce) cans sliced peaches, drained

10 to 12 bananas sliced (4 pounds)

3 cups mini marshmallows

3/4 cups chopped pecans (optional)

25 SERVINGS

2 (20-ounce) cans crushed pineapple

8 (15-ounce) cans mandarin oranges

4 large boxes instant lemon pudding

4 (29-ounce) cans sliced peaches, drained

8 pounds bananas, sliced

1 (1-pound) package mini marshmallows

1½ cups chopped pecans (optional)

50 SERVINGS

4 (20-ounce) cans crushed pineapple

16 (15-ounce) cans mandarin oranges, undrained

8 large boxes instant lemon pudding

8 (29-ounce) cans sliced peaches, drained

16 pounds bananas, sliced

2 (1-pound) packages mini marshmallows

3 cups chopped pecans (optional)

Drain juice from the pineapple and mandarin oranges into a large bowl. Stir in lemon pudding mix and whisk to blend well. Add the fruit and marshmallows and stir gently to combine. Fold in chopped pecans, if desired.

VARIATION: Substitute the mini marshmallows with half the measure of toasted coconut for a fun flavor change.

SCONES

12 SERVINGS
- 1½ cups sugar
- 3 packages dry yeast (about 2½ tablespoons)
- 4½ cups milk, warmed to about 105°F
- 11 cups (3 pounds) all-purpose flour
- 3 teaspoons salt
- Vegetable oil, for frying
- 1 pound butter
- 16 ounces honey

25 SERVINGS
- 3 cups sugar
- 6 packages dry yeast (⅓ cup)
- 1 quart plus 1 cup milk, warmed to about 105°F
- 6 pounds all-purpose flour
- 2 tablespoons salt
- Vegetable oil, for frying
- 2 pounds butter
- 32 ounces honey

50 SERVINGS
- 6 cups sugar
- ⅔ cup dry yeast
- 2½ quarts milk, warmed to about 105°F
- 12 pounds all-purpose flour
- 4 tablespoons salt
- Vegetable oil, for frying
- 4 pounds butter
- 64 ounces honey

EQUIPMENT
Camp stove
Large, deep, heavy skillet or Dutch oven (large recipe may require 2 skillets)

1. Dissolve sugar and yeast in the warm milk. Let stand for about 5 minutes to activate. Combine flour and salt in a large mixing bowl. Create a well in the top of the flour and pour in milk mixture while stirring. Continue stirring and kneading until a soft dough forms. If the mixture is too sticky to shape by hand, add flour little by little. Cover bowl and let the dough sit for 10 minutes in a warm area.

2. Heat the oil in a heavy skillet over medium-high heat until hot. If the oil smokes, it is too hot. By hand, pull balls of dough out of the bowl and stretch into a scone shape, about ½ inch thick. Fry in the oil, turning once, until golden on both sides. Place on paper towels to drain. Serve with butter and honey or make Navajo tacos with Tacorittos (see page 51) meat mixture.

EASY SLAW

12 SERVINGS
1½ cups mayonnaise
⅓ cup sugar
¼ cup apple cider
   vinegar
24 ounces shredded
   cabbage
½ teaspoon
   celery seed
½ teaspoon salt
½ teaspoon ground
   black pepper

25 SERVINGS
3 cups mayonnaise
⅔ cup sugar
½ cup apple cider
   vinegar
48 ounces shredded
   cabbage
1 teaspoon celery seed
1 teaspoon salt
1 teaspoon ground
   black pepper

50 SERVINGS
6 cups mayonnaise
1⅓ cups sugar
1 cup apple cider
   vinegar
96 ounces shredded
   cabbage
2 teaspoons
   celery seed
2 teaspoons salt
2 teaspoons ground
   black pepper

Mix all ingredients together in a large bowl and serve.

DUTCH OVEN

The Dutch oven is the original way to cook while camping, even when the early pioneers and settlers didn't know they were camping! With a Dutch oven, an entirely new world of hearty eating opens up. Foods can be baked with dry heat or braised with moisture, while the larger size of a Dutch oven makes it easy to cook enough food for most groups at one time. The basics of Dutch oven cooking can be mastered with a little practice and a healthy appetite.

FOUR-DAY DUTCH OVEN OUTFITTER MENU

DAY 1	DAY 2	DAY 3	DAY 4
DINNER	**BREAKFAST**	**BREAKFAST**	**BREAKFAST**
CURRY CHICKEN	EGG STRATA	BERRY BREAKFAST	INCREDIBLE BREAKFAST PIE
NO-FRIDGE FRUIT SALAD	QUICK CINNAMON ROLLS	FRESH FRUIT	MOUNTAIN MAN DONUTS
PINEAPPLE UPSIDE DOWN CAKE	**DINNER**	**DINNER**	
	SMOKY BRISKET	FIREMAN ENCHILADAS	
	COWBOY BEANS	FRESH PICO DE GALLO AND ICEBERG LETTUCE	
	EASY SLAW		
	OUTBACK ROLLS	PUMPKIN COBBLER	
	SODA POP COBBLER		

CLEANUP TIPS

A well-seasoned Dutch oven should be easy to clean. Simply remove as much food residue as possible and wipe with a paper towel with a little vegetable oil. For messier cleanup jobs, add warm water with a very small amount of mild dish soap. Too much detergent can remove the seasoning that protects cast iron.

A few tips can help with cleanup. Lining the bottom of the oven with strips of baking parchment paper that extend above the baked goods makes it easier to remove rolls, biscuits, cakes, and pies. Aluminum foil lining used judiciously can also make cleanup easier, although food that comes in direct contact with a well-seasoned Dutch oven is often more flavorful. Disposable aluminum Dutch oven liners also make cleanup a snap. Whatever you do, don't forget to apply a very light coat of vegetable oil or cast iron conditioner to all surfaces of the oven while it is still warm after washing. This will prevent the oven from rusting while it is stored.

CAST IRON USE AND CARE

Cast-iron cookware has been valued for its cooking properties for hundreds of years. Cast iron distributes heat evenly, resulting in cookware that is resistant to fluctuations in cooking temperature. It is also durable and can last for a lifetime if properly cared for.

It's important to make sure new cast-iron cookware is properly seasoned. While many manufacturers offer Dutch ovens and other cookware that are already seasoned, you may find a better value in seasoning the cast iron yourself. To season cast iron, heat up the Dutch oven or skillet in a hot fire or on an outdoor gas grill until very hot. Using a paper towel or basting brush, spread vegetable oil on all surfaces. Return the cookware to the heat to burn off the oil, changing the color of the metal from light gray to the black usually associated with a Dutch oven. Remove from heat and cool. While the oven is still warm, rub in a final very light coat of vegetable oil or cast iron conditioner over all surfaces.

PUSHING THE IRON ENVELOPE

After you have a little experience, push the boundaries of Dutch oven cooking by adapting recipes from home. Master Dutch oven chefs are able to create five-course meals, all cooked in cast iron. Dutch ovens and cast iron also work great at home in the oven, allowing you to practice recipes before heading out into the wild.

You may want to add special tools to your gear if you plan to cook in a Dutch oven frequently. A lid-removal tool is handy for quick checks on the food. A trivet lid holder allows you to present and serve your Dutch oven dish on the lid of the oven. A Dutch oven charcoal stand brings the cooking up to waist level for convenience.

For those interested in backpacking, canoe or kayak touring, or horse packing, many manufacturers sell lightweight cast-aluminum Dutch ovens. A small 8-inch oven is great for short backpack trips and opens up a whole range of possibilities. Aluminum also has the advantage of not needing to be seasoned.

COOKING AT THE RIGHT TEMPERATURE

DUTCH OVEN	325°	350°	375°	400°	425°	450°
8-inch	15	16	17	18	19	20
briquettes on top/bottom	10/5	11/5	11/6	12/6	13/6	14/6
10-inch	19	21	23	25	27	29
briquettes on top/bottom	13/6	14/7	16/7	17/8	18/9	19/10
12-inch	23	25	27	29	31	33
briquettes on top/bottom	16/7	17/8	18/9	19/10	21/10	22/11
14-inch	30	32	34	36	38	40
briquettes on top/bottom	20/10	21/11	22/12	24/12	25/13	26/14

While you certainly can use a Dutch oven right in the coals from a traditional wood campfire, most backwoods chefs find charcoal briquettes easier to use for maintaining consistent temperatures. The number of briquettes determines the temperature. Each recipe specifies how many briquettes you'll need, or refer to the chart above, provided by Lodge Cast Iron. Weather conditions and the air temperature can affect the heat generated by the briquettes, so be sure to watch how your food is cooking and make adjustments as needed by adding or removing one or two coals.

You may find that a chimney-style briquette igniter helps you create hotter charcoal to work with much faster.

ICEBOX COOKING METHOD

An easy way to minimize the amount of time spent preparing food on a campout is to prepare ingredients at home and package them in gallon-size resealable bags. Store the bags of ingredients in an ice chest, ready to be combined to make recipes. This method works especially well for Dutch oven dishes. Many ingredients can be frozen beforehand in resealable bags and placed in the cooler to help maintain a safe temperature for refrigerated foods. It's also often easy to pre-cook ground beef mixtures at home and pack them refrigerated or frozen. Recipes in this cookbook that are well suited to the icebox method of preparation are marked with this special symbol.

ICEBOX COOKING METHOD SEE P. 65

EGG STRATA

SERVES 6 TO 8

10 slices hearty white
  bread (stale bread
  works well)
1/4 cup butter, softened
8 ounces shredded
  Mexican-style cheese
12 eggs beaten
2 cups half-and-half
2 cups milk
2 teaspoons salt

1/2 teaspoon ground
  black pepper
1/4 teaspoon paprika
1 tablespoon prepared
  yellow mustard
1 teaspoon
  Worcestershire sauce
2 cups chopped
  mushrooms

EQUIPMENT
Charcoal briquettes
  or campfire coals
12-inch Dutch oven, 10
  coals on bottom, 16
  coals on top, 350°F

1. Butter one side of each bread slice. Cut bread slices into fourths. Layer half the bread in the bottom of a Dutch oven, butter side down. Sprinkle with half of the cheese. Layer the remaining bread over top and sprinkle with the remaining cheese.

2. Combine the remaining ingredients and mix well. Pour egg mixture over bread. Cover and place in the cooler for at least 2 hours and preferably overnight.

3. Bake with heat on top and bottom for 1 hour, covered. Let stand for 10 minutes before slicing and serving.

QUICK CINNAMON ROLLS

SERVES 6 TO 8

1 loaf frozen bread
  dough, thawed
  (substitute Outback
  Rolls dough [page
  84] if you prefer to
  make from scratch)
1 stick butter, melted
1 cup brown sugar

1 teaspoon cinnamon
1/2 cup chopped pecans
1 cup raisins (optional)

GLAZE
2 cups powdered sugar
2 to 4 tablespoons milk
1/2 teaspoon
  vanilla extract

EQUIPMENT
Parchment paper
Charcoal briquettes
  or campfire coals
12-inch Dutch oven, 10
  coals on bottom, 16
  coals on top, 350°F

1. Roll out bread dough out lengthwise on a sheet of parchment paper or wax paper until it is about 10 inches wide by 20 inches long. Spread with melted butter, sugar, cinnamon, pecans, and raisins, if desired. Roll up from the long edge and cut rolls into 1 1/2-inch sections.

2. Place the rolls in a greased Dutch oven and allow to rise in a warm area for about 1 hour. Bake with heat on top and bottom for 20 to 25 minutes.

3. Prepare glaze by whisking together the powdered sugar, milk, and vanilla, adding more milk 1 tablespoon at a time to reach your desired consistency. Drizzle over hot cinnamon rolls and serve.

BERRY BREAKFAST

SERVES 6 TO 8

2 cups all-purpose
   flour
2 eggs, beaten
1 teaspoon baking
   powder
1 cup sour cream
1/2 teaspoon
   baking soda
1/2 cup sugar

1/2 cup butter, melted
1 cup raspberries or
   boysenberries
3/4 cup brown sugar
Boysenberry
   pancake syrup
Whipped cream
   (optional)

EQUIPMENT
Charcoal briquettes
   or campfire coals
12-inch Dutch oven, 10
   coals on bottom, 16
   coals on top, 350°F

Combine all ingredients in a mixing bowl except berries and brown sugar and mix until moist throughout. Gently fold in the berries and pour into a 12-inch Dutch oven. Top with brown sugar. Bake with heat on top and bottom for 40 minutes. Serve warm with boysenberry syrup and whipped cream.

INCREDIBLE BREAKFAST PIE

SERVES 6 TO 8

1 refrigerated piecrust
(or 1 package
piecrust mix,
prepared according
to directions)
8 slices cooked
bacon, crumbled
1 cup shredded
cheddar cheese
1½ cups milk

½ cup all-
purpose flour
1 teaspoon salt
2 green onions,
finely diced
1 tablespoon fresh
or dried parsley
8 eggs, beaten
Ketchup or salsa

EQUIPMENT
Charcoal briquettes
or campfire coals
10-inch Dutch oven, 8
coals on bottom, 14
coals on top, 350°F
Parchment paper

1. Line the bottom of a 10-inch Dutch oven with strips of folded parchment paper up the side of the oven to aid in removing the pie. Unroll the piecrust and place it in the bottom of the oven, stretching it up the sides. Pinch the edges between your thumb and forefinger to scallop them.

2. Sprinkle bacon and cheese on the bottom of the piecrust. Add milk, flour, salt, green onions, and parsley to the beaten eggs and mix well. Pour egg mixture into the piecrust.

3. Cover and bake with heat on top and bottom for 45 minutes, until eggs are set. Let the pie cool for 10 minutes before lifting it out. Serve with ketchup or salsa.

DUTCH OVEN POTATOES

SERVES 6 TO 8

1 stick butter
1/2 cup water
2 tablespoons fresh
  or dried parsley
1 tablespoon chopped
  rosemary

1/2 teaspoon ground
  black pepper
12 red potatoes,
  quartered
1 small onion, diced

EQUIPMENT
Charcoal briquettes
  or campfire coals
12-inch Dutch oven, 10
  coals on bottom, 16
  coals on top, 350°F

1. Heat Dutch oven over coals, adding butter to melt. Add water, herbs, and black pepper. Stir in potatoes and onions and evenly coat.

2. Cover and cook for 45 minutes with heat on top and bottom, stirring halfway through, until the potatoes are tender and brown.

COWBOY BEANS

SERVES 6 TO 8

8 slices bacon
1 tablespoon flour
1 small onion, chopped
2 (15.5-ounce) cans
   pinto beans

2 (15.5-ounce) cans
   kidney beans
2 pints chicken stock
$\frac{1}{2}$ teaspoon sage
$\frac{1}{2}$ teaspoon thyme

EQUIPMENT
Charcoal briquettes
   or campfire coals
12-inch Dutch oven, 18
   coals on bottom, no
   coals on top, 350°F

1. Heat the Dutch oven over the coals. Fry bacon until cooked and then crumble; drain off any grease, reserving 1 to 2 tablespoons in the oven. Add flour and stir to form a smooth paste, cooking until light brown. Add onions and cook for 3 more minutes, until translucent.

2. Add remaining ingredients and continue simmering covered for another 30 minutes, until thickened.

CURRY CHICKEN

SERVES 6 TO 8

1 tablespoon olive
  or vegetable oil
1½ pounds chicken
  breast, cut into strips
2 (13.5-ounce) cans
  coconut milk
4 to 6 tablespoons
  yellow curry paste
1 (8-ounce) can
  bamboo shoots,
  drained

1 (8-ounce) package
  frozen peas
  and carrots
½ cup fresh basil
  (substitute 2
  tablespoons
  dried basil)
2 potatoes, cubed
5 cups water
2 cups uncooked
  white rice

EQUIPMENT
Charcoal briquettes
  or campfire coals
12-inch Dutch oven, 8
  coals on bottom, 14
  coals on top, 325°F

1. Heat Dutch oven over coals and add oil. Add chicken strips, cooking about 5 minutes while stirring to brown. Add additional ingredients and stir to mix well.

2. Cover and cook for 35 to 45 minutes with heat on top and bottom, until rice has absorbed much of the liquid.

BISCUITS AND GRAVY

SERVES 6 TO 8

3 cups biscuit mix (Bisquick)

3 cups milk, divided

1 pound ground breakfast sausage

2 tablespoons dried onion flakes

4 tablespoons flour

2 cubes chicken bouillon

1 teaspoon ground black pepper

EQUIPMENT

Parchment paper

Charcoal briquettes or campfire coals

12-inch Dutch oven, 10 coals on bottom, 16 coals on top, 350°F

1. Mix biscuit mix with 1 cup of milk, reserving 2 cups. Roll out dough on a floured surface and cut out biscuits with a glass or biscuit cutter. Place in a Dutch oven that has been prepared with folded strips of parchment paper so that biscuits can easily be removed.

2. Bake for 10 to 15 minutes until golden brown with heat on top and bottom, until golden brown. Remove biscuits and return Dutch oven to the fire without the lid.

3. Brown sausage and onion flakes until cooked. Drain off most of the fat, reserving a few tablespoons in the Dutch oven. Add flour slowly while stirring to make a smooth paste. Add the remaining 2 cups of milk and almost bring to a boil. Add chicken bouillon and ground black pepper and cook for about 5 minutes. Thin, if necessary, with additional milk. Serve sausage gravy over biscuits.

LEMON–LIME TURKEY STEAK

SERVES 6 TO 8

ICEBOX COOKING METHOD — SEE P. 65

6 to 8 turkey breast
  steaks (about
  2 pounds)
1 (12-ounce) can
  lemon-lime soda
2 tablespoons
  lemon juice

2 tablespoons
  soy sauce
2 tablespoons
  melted butter
1 teaspoon ginger
Hot prepared rice
  (optional)

EQUIPMENT
Charcoal briquettes
  or campfire coals
12-inch Dutch oven, 10
  coals on bottom, 16
  coals on top, 350°F

1. Place all ingredients in a gallon-size resealable freezer bag and marinate for at least 4 hours or overnight.

2. When ready to cook, pour the contents from the freezer bag into a 12-inch Dutch oven and cook with heat on top and bottom for 30 minutes. Serve over rice or with Dutch Oven Potatoes (see page 73).

ICEBOX COOKING METHOD — SEE P. 65 —

FIREMAN ENCHILADAS

SERVES 6 TO 8

1 pound ground beef
1 small onion, chopped
2 bell peppers, green
 or red, chopped
1 (4-ounce) can diced
 green chiles
1 (10-ounce) can
 enchilada sauce
3 (15.5-ounce) cans
 pinto beans,
 undrained

2 (28-ounce) cans
 diced tomatoes
1 (4.25-ounce) can
 sliced olives
6 to 8 flour tortillas
3 cups shredded
 cheddar cheese
Sour cream

EQUIPMENT
Charcoal briquettes
 or campfire coals
12-inch Dutch oven, 10
 coals on bottom, 16
 coals on top, 350°F

1. Heat Dutch oven over coals and brown the ground beef and onions until cooked through. Drain off any excess fat. Add remaining ingredients except for tortillas, cheese and sour cream. Simmer for about 10 minutes and remove to a separate bowl.

2. To assemble enchiladas, dip each tortilla in the mixture's sauce to coat. Fill with meat and beans and roll up, placing each enchilada back into the Dutch oven. Top with cheese. Bake with heat on top and bottom for about 30 to 40 minutes, until hot throughout. Serve with sour cream.

PIONEER PIZZA

SERVES 6 TO 8

2 tablespoons
  cornmeal
1 loaf frozen bread
  dough, thawed
  (substitute Outback
  Rolls dough,
  page 84)
1 (10-ounce) bottle
  barbecue sauce

16 ounces shredded
  mozzarella or pizza
  blend cheese
1 (8-ounce) package
  cooked, sliced
  chicken breast
1 small red onion,
  diced
1/2 cup fresh cilantro,
  loosely chopped

EQUIPMENT
Charcoal briquettes
  or campfire coals
12-inch Dutch oven, 14
  coals on bottom, 16
  coals on top, 400°F

1. Sprinkle cornmeal in the bottom of a 12-inch or larger Dutch oven. Roll or stretch out bread dough to fit the bottom of the Dutch oven and set in place.

2. Spread barbecue sauce on dough, followed by cheese, chicken, red onions, and fresh cilantro. Bake with heat on top and bottom for 15 to 20 minutes.

SMOKY BRISKET

SERVES 6 TO 8

1 package dry
   onion soup mix
1 (12-ounce) jar
   chili sauce
1 (12-ounce) can
   regular Dr. Pepper

1/4 teaspoon natural
   liquid smoke
1 (4- to 5-pound)
   beef brisket

EQUIPMENT
Charcoal briquettes
   or campfire coals
12-inch Dutch oven, 10
   coals on bottom, 16
   coals on top, 350°F

In a bowl, combine all ingredients except brisket. Place brisket fat side up in a Dutch oven and pour sauce over the top. Bake with heat on top and bottom for 45 minutes per pound of meat. Every hour or so, you may need to restock with hot coals.

ROCKY MOUNTAIN MEATBALLS

SERVES 6 TO 8

2 pounds ground beef

1 envelope dry
onion soup mix

1/2 cup cracker crumbs

3 eggs, beaten

1 tablespoon
vegetable oil

1 small onion, sliced

4 large potatoes,
sliced into rounds

2 (10.75-ounce) cans
condensed cream
of mushroom soup

2 cups sour cream

Salt

Ground black pepper

EQUIPMENT

Charcoal briquettes
or campfire coals

12-inch Dutch oven, 10
coals on bottom, 16
coals on top, 350°F

1. Combine ground beef, soup mix, cracker crumbs, and eggs, mixing well. Form into 2-inch balls. Heat oil in a Dutch oven until hot, add onions and meatballs, cooking until the outsides of the meatballs are brown and onions are softened.

2. Drain off any excess oil. Add potatoes and cover with mushroom soup and sour cream, stirring to coat. Season with salt and black pepper to taste. Bake with heat on top and bottom for 45 minutes.

OUTBACK ROLLS

SERVES 6 TO 8

¼ cup butter
¼ cup water
1 cup milk
⅓ cup sugar

1 package yeast
2 eggs, beaten
1 teaspoon salt
4½ cups flour

EQUIPMENT
Charcoal briquettes
 or campfire coals
12-inch Dutch oven, 14
 coals on bottom, 20
 coals on top, 450°F
Small saucepan

1. Melt butter in a small saucepan. Add water, milk, and sugar, continuing to cook until warm, about 105°F. Remove from heat and add yeast. Wait 5 to 10 minutes for yeast to activate and foam. Add eggs and stir.

2. In a large mixing bowl, combine salt and flour. Add the liquid ingredients and stir to create a soft dough. Knead for 5 minutes and cover. Let the dough rise for 20 minutes in a warm place.

3. Punch down dough and form into 18 to 20 balls. Place in a warm Dutch oven and allow to rise for 20 minutes. Bake with heat on top and bottom for 15 to 18 minutes. Brush tops of the rolls with butter while warm.

PUMPKIN COBBLER

SERVES 6 TO 8

1 (30-ounce) can
    pumpkin
1 cup sugar
3 eggs, beaten
2 teaspoons pumpkin
    pie spice
3/4 teaspoon salt

1 (12-ounce) can
    evaporated milk
1/2 cup butter, melted
1 box yellow cake mix
1/2 cup chopped
    pecans (optional)
Whipped cream
    or ice cream

EQUIPMENT
Charcoal briquettes
    or campfire coals
12-inch Dutch oven, 10
    coals on bottom, 16
    coals on top, 350°F

1. In a Dutch oven, combine pumpkin, sugar, eggs, pumpkin pie spice, salt and evaporated milk. Mix well.

2. In a small mixing bowl, use a fork to cut melted butter into the cake mix. Add pecans, if desired.

3. Spread cake mix topping over pumpkin. Bake with heat on top and bottom for 50 to 60 minutes. Serve topped with whipped cream or ice cream.

PINEAPPLE UPSIDE DOWN CAKE

SERVES 6 TO 8

1 (8-ounce) can
 pineapple rings,
 drained
1/4 cup brown sugar

1 box lemon cake mix
1 cup powdered sugar
1/4 cup orange juice

EQUIPMENT
Charcoal briquettes
 or campfire coals
12-inch Dutch oven, 10
 coals on bottom, 16
 coals on top, 350°F
Parchment paper

1. Layer pineapple rings in the bottom of a Dutch oven that has been prepared with strips of parchment paper. Sprinkle with brown sugar. Prepare cake mix according to package directions and pour batter over pineapple.

2. Bake with heat on top and bottom for 25 to 30 minutes. While cake is baking, mix powdered sugar with orange juice to form a smooth glaze. When cake is done and still hot, poke holes in the top and pour glaze across the cake.

3. Turn Dutch oven upside down to release cake onto a serving dish.

SODA POP COBBLER

SERVES 6 TO 8

1 box yellow cake mix
2 (21-ounce) cans
   favorite pie filling
   (peach, raspberry,
   apple or blueberry
   works well)

1 (12-ounce) can
   favorite soda
   (orange, root
   beer, lemon-lime,
   strawberry, cola)
Whipped cream

EQUIPMENT
Charcoal briquettes
   or campfire coals
12-inch Dutch oven, 10
   coals on bottom, 16
   coals on top, 350°F

Place pie filling in the bottom of a greased Dutch oven. Cover with dry cake mix. Pour soda over cake mix, covering entirely. Let stand for 30 minutes before baking with heat on top and bottom for 45 to 55 minutes. Serve with whipped cream.

MOUNTAIN MAN DONUTS

MAKES ABOUT 2 DOZEN

1 cup boiling water
3/4 cup instant mashed
   potato flakes
3/4 cup warm milk
1 package yeast
1/4 cup melted butter
1/4 cup sugar
1 egg

1/2 teaspoon salt
4 cups flour
Vegetable oil, for frying
2 cups powdered sugar
2 to 4 tablespoons
   water
1/2 teaspoon
   vanilla extract

EQUIPMENT
Charcoal briquettes
   or campfire coals
12-inch Dutch
   oven, 12 coals on
   bottom, 375°F

1. In a small mixing bowl, add boiling water to potato flakes to reconstitute. In a larger mixing bowl, combine milk, yeast, butter, and sugar. Allow to rest until yeast activates and turns foamy.

2. Add the egg to milk mixture, whisking to beat. Add the mashed potatoes, salt, and flour one cup and a time, stirring until a soft dough is formed. Dough should be soft and slightly sticky. Allow to rest covered in a warm place until doubled in size.

3. On a floured surface, roll out dough to 1/2-inch thickness and cut with a doughnut cutter or the top of a glass. Cut out centers with a narrow bottle mouth or cap to form donuts.

4. Heat 2 to 3 inches of oil in a Dutch oven and fry donuts a few at a time until golden brown. Mix the powdered sugar with water and vanilla extract to form a glaze, and coat the donuts.

CAMP GOURMET

So you've mastered camp cooking so far and are ready for hot and haute cuisine? The following recipes are designed to inspire your inner celebrity chef and allow you to show off your mastery of outdoor cooking. Allow your imagination and taste buds to take you to new altitudes of camp taste.

GOURMET THREE-DAY MENU

DAY 1	DAY 2	DAY 3
DINNER	**BREAKFAST**	**BREAKFAST**
TINFOIL BISTRO MARINARA MEATBALLS	SAUSAGE AND PEPPER BREAKFAST BURRITOS	SOURDOUGH PANCAKES
TINFOIL GARLIC BREAD (FROM PIZZA PITA WITH GARLIC BREAD)	FRESH FRUIT	VANILLA RICE PUDDING
BERRY PIE	**LUNCH**	
	GREEN APPLE AND CRANBERRY SALAD	
	CRUSTY FRENCH BREAD	
	DINNER	
	MANICOTTI	
	MIXED GREENS	
	SHEPHERD CHEESE BREAD WITH ROASTED GARLIC SPREAD	
	ICE CREAM IN A JAR	

THE SPICE RACK

To really unleash your creativity as a camp cook, you'll need to bring along a portable spice rack. Often dollar or discount stores will carry extra-small spice jars, which are great for occasional camp cooking. A basic spice rack should include ground black pepper, garlic powder, dried parsley, Italian seasoning, sage, thyme, nutmeg, cinnamon, chili powder, lemon pepper, and cayenne pepper. Make a note of which spices you use frequently at home and add them to your collection. A small tool or tackle box with a deep gear tray makes a great portable spice rack that is easy to use.

Fresh herbs and spices add special flavor and are often over-looked. When filling your ice chest, don't forget to add fresh cilantro, basil, and Italian parsley. Fresh rosemary is particularly useful to impart an outdoor flavor to foods.

OPEN-FIRE GRILLING

Many campgrounds have fires with metal grates for cooking. Outdoor stores also sell portable fire grates. While creating a good bed of coals for grilling over an open fire takes practice, cooking on a grate is a great way to add flavor to meats. Keep in mind that hardwoods impart the best flavor while many soft woods may have off-taste smoke due to their high sap content if the wood isn't properly seasoned. One alternative is to bring along a bag of mesquite or hickory hardwood chips to sprinkle over a low bed of coals.

MATCHING FOODS TO THE SCENERY

Camping is a great way to experience the beauty of nature. Planning menus with dishes to enhance the experience can be a lot of fun. Think about the environment in which you'll be as well as the weather. The American Southwest lends itself per-fectly to foods inspired by the flavors of Mexico, while camping in cooler temperate forests may call for warm and earthy com-fort foods. If fishing is a part of your vacation plans or you'll be camping in coastal areas, plan to cook fresh dishes with local ingredients. Often on the way to your campsite, you'll pass through small towns. Check out the local markets for seasonal specialties that can be incorporated into your meals.

SOURDOUGH PANCAKES

SERVES 4

1 cup sourdough
  starter
2 cups unbleached
  all-purpose flour

1 egg, beaten
2 tablespoons sugar
1/2 teaspoon salt
2 cups buttermilk

EQUIPMENT
Camp stove
Griddle

1. Combine all ingredients in a mixing bowl and stir gently. Don't overmix. The batter should be slightly lumpy. Pour onto a lightly greased griddle heated over medium-high heat and cook pancakes, Flipping once bubbles have burst.

2. Serve with butter and warm maple syrup.

VARIATION: Mix in blueberries, diced bananas or diced apples, and a pinch of cinnamon.

SOURDOUGH STARTER

SERVES 4

1 package yeast
1 teaspoon sugar

2 cups warm water
2 cups flour

Dissolve yeast and sugar in the warm water. Set aside for 5 minutes, until bubbly. Mix in flour, one cup at a time, until a sticky dough forms. Place in a glass jar (not metal), cover loosely, and leave out at room temperature for 3 to 4 days, until bubbly. Refrigerate. When you use 1 cup of starter, replace with 1 cup each of water and flour and leave out at room temperature to allow the starter to ferment again before refrigerating.

SAUSAGE AND PEPPER BREAKFAST BURRITOS

SERVES 4 TO 6

1 pound chorizo
   sausage
2 potatoes, diced
1 red bell pepper, sliced
1 orange bell
   pepper, sliced

8 ounces Cotija
   cheese, crumbled
Salsa
8 to 10 tortillas

EQUIPMENT
Camp stove or
   campfire coals
Skillet or Dutch oven

1. Crumble the sausage and add it to a skillet along with the diced potatoes. Cook for about 10 minutes over medium-high heat, until sausage is browned and potatoes are soft. Add bell pepper slices, cooking until soft. Top with crumbled Cotija cheese and set aside, keeping warm.

2. Warm each tortilla briefly in the skillet, then fill with the sausage mixture and top with salsa, as desired.

TINFOIL BISTRO

EACH RECIPE SERVES 1

ASIAN CHICKEN

1 boneless skinless
    chicken breast
1/4 cup teriyaki sauce
1/4 cup orange juice
2 cups frozen stir-
    fry vegetables

SWEDISH BAKE

6 or 7 frozen Swedish
    meatballs, thawed
1/4 cup beef
    consommé soup
1/2 cup sour cream
2 red or new
    potatoes, diced
Dash ground
    black pepper
Dash allspice
Dash nutmeg

SEAFOOD STEAMER

3 or 4 fresh Manila
    clams, scrubbed
3 or 4 fresh mussels,
    scrubbed
3 large uncooked
    shrimp, peeled
    and deveined
1 firm fish fillet, such
    as halibut or mahi-
    mahi, cut into
    2-inch chunks
2 red or new
    potatoes, diced
1/2 cup chicken broth
4 tablespoons
    melted butter
1 teaspoon minced
    garlic

IRISH ROAST

1 thick slice of
    cooked or canned
    corned beef
1/4 head cabbage
2 red potatoes, diced
Ground black pepper

COWBOY BBQ

3 thin slices uncooked
    beef brisket or
    flank steak
1/4 cup mesquite
    barbecue sauce
1 small onion, sliced
1 baking potato,
    sliced with skin on

MARINARA MEATBALLS

6 or 7 frozen Italian
    meatballs, thawed
1 cup bottled
    marinara sauce
1/4 cup grated
    Parmesan cheese
1 cup fresh ravioli
    or tortellini

For twists on the classic foil dinner, try the following combinations. Combine all ingredients for your chosen variation and wrap in foil using the butcher's wrap method (see page 10). Cook on the coals for 10 minutes per side.

VANILLA RICE PUDDING

SERVES 4 TO 6

2 cups water
2 cups instant rice
2 (12-ounce) cans
   evaporated milk
1/2 teaspoon salt
1/4 cup butter

3/4 cup sugar
1 teaspoon vanilla
   extract
1 teaspoon nutmeg
3 eggs, beaten

EQUIPMENT
Camp stove
Heavy saucepan

1. Bring water to a boil in a heavy saucepan. Slowly add rice. Cover and simmer for 8 to 10 minutes, until rice is soft.

2. Add milk, salt, and butter to the rice and bring to a boil. Reduce heat and simmer for 5 minutes. Add sugar, vanilla, and nutmeg to the beaten eggs. Slowly pour the egg mixture into the rice, stirring constantly until rice thickens. Allow to cool slightly and serve for breakfast or dessert.

TROUT FLORENTINE

SERVES 2

2 trout, cleaned
   and dressed
½ cup dry
   breadcrumbs
2 tablespoons
   butter, melted
2 cups fresh baby
   spinach leaves,
   chopped

1 teaspoon diced garlic
3 green onions,
   thinly sliced
½ cup chicken
   broth or stock
1 teaspoon lemon juice
Salt
Ground black pepper

EQUIPMENT
Campfire coals
Heavy-duty
   aluminum foil

1. Place each trout on a sheet of aluminum foil, shiny side facing up. Mix the breadcrumbs with the melted butter and stuff each trout. Continue stuffing with spinach, garlic, and green onions. Drizzle stuffing with chicken broth and lemon juice. Add a dash of salt and black pepper. Wrap in foil and cook over the coals for 6 minutes per side.

2. Alternately, sauté each stuffed trout in a skillet over medium heat with 1 cup of chicken stock and 2 teaspoons of garlic.

ICEBOX COOKING METHOD
- SEE P. 65 -

GREEN APPLE AND CRANBERRY SALAD

SERVES 2 TO 4

1/4 cup mayonnaise
2 tablespoons
   lemon juice
1/2 teaspoon salt
2 crisp green apples,
   cored and chopped
1/2 cup candied walnuts
1 cup dried cranberries

In a mixing bowl, whisk together mayonnaise and lemon juice. Add remaining ingredients and stir gently to coat.

TERIYAKI BEEF

SERVES 2 TO 4

¹/₄ cup soy sauce
¹/₂ cup water
1 teaspoon ground
   ginger

¹/₂ teaspoon garlic
   powder
¹/₄ cup brown sugar

1 pound flat-iron
   or flank steak

1. Combine all ingredients in a gallon-size resealable freezer bag and marinate for at least 4 hours or preferably overnight.

2. On a hot grill over a fire or charcoal, grill steak for 6 to 8 minutes per side, until slightly charred on the outside. Slice and serve with vegetables and rice.

MANICOTTI

SERVES 6 TO 8

1 (16-ounce) container
   ricotta cheese
2 tablespoons Italian
   seasoning, divided
1 egg, beaten
1 (24-ounce) can
   Italian-style
   stewed tomatoes
2 (8-ounce) cans
   tomato sauce

2 teaspoons sugar
1 teaspoon salt
2 small zucchini,
   thickly chopped
1 (8-ounce) package
   uncooked
   manicotti shells
1/2 cup water
16 ounces shredded
   mozzarella cheese

EQUIPMENT
Charcoal briquettes
   or campfire coals
12-inch Dutch oven, 10
   coals on bottom, 16
   coals on top, 350°F

1. Mix together ricotta cheese, 1 tablespoon of Italian seasoning, and egg. Add stewed tomatoes and tomato sauce to the bottom of a Dutch oven. Stir in sugar, salt, and remaining 1 tablespoon of Italian seasoning. Add the chopped zucchini.

2. Stuff each manicotti shell with the ricotta cheese mixture. Place the stuffed shells in the tomato mixture. Add water, but don't stir. Make sure manicotti shells are covered with water or sauce. Cover with mozzarella cheese and bake with heat on top and bottom for 40 to 45 minutes, until the noodles are soft.

SHEPHERD CHEESE BREAD WITH ROASTED GARLIC SPREAD

SERVES 6 TO 8

3 or 4 heads garlic

3 to 4 tablespoons olive oil

1 round loaf white or sourdough bread, unsliced

$1/2$ cup butter, melted

1 cup shredded Gruyère cheese

1 cup shredded sharp cheddar cheese

EQUIPMENT

Campfire coals

Heavy-duty aluminum foil

1. Peel away the outer dry skin from the garlic cloves, leaving the head intact. Cut off the top $1/2$ inch of the cloves, exposing the garlic inside. Drizzle a tablespoon of olive oil over each head and wrap in aluminum foil. Roast on the coals for 15 to 20 minutes or until the garlic feels soft when squeezed.

2. While the garlic is roasting, cut three-quarters of the way through the bread in 1-inch increments lengthwise and widthwise, creating a checkerboard appearance. Pour the melted butter over the bread and stuff cheeses in between the slices. Wrap the loaf in foil and place on the coals, cooking for 10 to 15 minutes, until the cheeses are melted. Remove roasted garlic from their skins and spread over the bread while warm.

JAPANESE-STYLE VEGETABLES

SERVES 2 TO 4

1 (12-ounce) bag shelled frozen edamame
2 cups baby carrots
1 small onion, chopped

¼ cup rice wine vinegar
¼ cup water
½ teaspoon salt

EQUIPMENT
Charcoal briquettes, campfire coals, or camp stove
12-inch Dutch oven, 10 coals on bottom, 16 coals on top, 350°F

Place ingredients in a Dutch oven and cook with heat on top and bottom for 20 minutes.

BERRY PIE

SERVES 8

PIECRUST
4 cups flour
2 teaspoons salt
¼ cup butter
1 cup shortening
¼ to ⅓ cup water

FILLING
4 tablespoons all-
  purpose flour
1¼ cups sugar
1 teaspoon almond
  extract

1 teaspoon vanilla
  extract
2 teaspoons
  lemon juice
1 (16-ounce) package
  frozen or fresh
  raspberries, thawed
1 (16-ounce) package
  frozen or fresh sliced
  strawberries, thawed
4 tablespoons
  butter, melted
1 egg, beaten
Coarse sugar

EQUIPMENT
Charcoal briquettes
  or campfire coals
12-inch Dutch oven, 10
  coals on bottom, 16
  coals on top, 350°F

1. Using a fork, cut the flour and salt into the butter and shortening until crumbly. Add the water a little at a time, until a dough forms. Try to not overwork the dough. Cover with plastic wrap and chill.

2. For the filling, mix flour and sugar together in a bowl. Add extracts and lemon juice and gently fold in berries.

3. Separate dough into 2 balls and roll out both crusts to ¼ inch thick. Place a crust in the bottom of the Dutch oven, pulling it at least halfway up the side. Add the berry mixture and cover with the remaining piecrust or cut into strips to form a lattice top. Pinch the edges between your thumb and forefinger to scallop. Add the melted butter to the beaten egg and brush the top with the mixture. Sprinkle with coarse sugar.

4. Cover and bake with heat on top and bottom for about 30 minutes, until the crust is brown and the filling is bubbly.

ICE CREAM IN A JAR

SERVES 2 TO 4

1½ cups cream
½ cup milk
½ cup sugar
3 tablespoons instant
vanilla pudding

½ teaspoon
vanilla extract
Fruit, nuts, candy bars,
cookies, or other
mix-ins as desired

EQUIPMENT
Large mixing bowl
filled with ice
1-quart jar or water
bottle with lid
1 box rock or
kosher salt

1. Combine all ingredients and pour into the 1-quart container.

2. Sprinkle rock salt in layers throughout the ice in the large mixing bowl. Place the container with the ice cream ingredients in the center of the ice, covering well. Take turns spinning and turning the container. About every 5 minutes, remove the lid and scrape frozen ice cream off the sides. In about 30 to 40 minutes, the ice cream should be ready to serve. The longer it's left in ice, the firmer the ice cream will be.

BACK-PACKING

I f camping is getting back to nature, back-packing takes it up a notch, really allowing a person to become a part of nature. You're on the trail, often miles away from the stress of modern life, reliant on only what you can carry for shelter and food. Cooking well for groups while backpacking presents unique challenges. Look to the following recipes for ideas and inspiration.

THREE-DAY BACKPACK MENU

DAY 1	DAY 2	DAY 3
LUNCH	**BREAKFAST**	**BREAKFAST**
AVOCADO BACON WRAP	BREAKFAST WRAPS	HIKER'S CEREAL
GORP	SWEET MIX	**LUNCH**
DINNER	**LUNCH**	PIZZA BAGEL
MASALA CHICKEN AND RICE	PITA SANDWICH	**DINNER**
FRESH FRUIT	**DINNER**	TOMATO NOODLES
	SPLIT PEA SOUP	PARMESAN AND OLIVE OIL COUSCOUS
	CHEESY BREAD	
	CARAMEL CHEESECAKE DESSERT	

ALTITUDE CONSIDERATIONS

While an often-quoted research study on airline food suggested that taste buds are dulled by at high altitudes, my experience, as well as anecdotal evidence, suggests the opposite to be true. When on extended backpacking trips above 8,000 feet, I've found those in my group tend to be more sensitive to spicy flavors. Whether this is due to the drier air or less oxygen, I'm not sure.

Water boils at a lower temperature for every foot above sea level you travel, meaning foods cook slower. At extreme altitudes, foods such as pasta may not cook at all. Take this into consideration when planning for fuel requirements.

GROUPS AND BACKPACKING

Backpacking in a group presents special challenges. The more people in a group, the greater the stress on the environment when setting up camp. It's more difficult to purify enough water and take care of sanitation needs, and cooking for more than two or three people with lightweight backpacking stoves is also a challenge.

Ideally, a backpacking group should be made up of six or fewer people. Plan on having one stove per two people. While cooking systems do exist for up to four people, you are often limited to just boiling water for rehydrating freeze-dried meals. It's important to allow for one water-purification system per two people. Usually one person carries the stove and the other carries the water-purification system.

GROCERY STORE MEALS

While freeze-dried backpacking meals are lightweight and relatively easy to prepare, they do have drawbacks. They can be expensive and also tend to be overseasoned, especially when eaten at altitude or on extended trips. By creating menus from ingredients found at the grocery store, you can save money and tailor your meals to your tastes. Ingredients can be packaged in resealable bags and prepared in advance—just like commercial freeze-dried food.

COOKING SYSTEMS

Backpacking and mountaineering cooking systems have advanced tremendously in the last decade. While liquid fuel–based and gas canister–based systems are still the two dominant types of stoves, integrated systems have arrived on the market that feature cooking vessels engineered to be mated to a dedicated stove for increased efficiency.

What type of stove you buy is best determined by your cooking style. Integrated systems such as the Jetboil and the MSR Reactor are very lightweight and are primarily designed to boil water quickly. This is also important when melting snow. The older-style backpacking stoves are less efficient at boiling water and are heavier, but they are generally more versatile for other types of cooking, such as sautéing and frying.

HIKER'S CEREAL

SERVES 1 TO 2

2 cups granola
1/3 cup dry
   powdered milk

1/2 cup dried
   cranberries
1/4 cup brown sugar

1 cup cold water

Pack all ingredients in a quart-size resealable freezer bag. When ready to prepare, add the cold water and shake. Put everything into a bowl—or eat it straight out of the bag.

Use your imagination to add other dried fruits, nuts, and spices to the mix to create your own custom breakfast bowl.

GORP

MAKES 11 CUPS

4 cups Cheerios
2 cups raisins

2 cups salted peanuts
2 cups M&M candies

1 cup chocolate chips

Combine all ingredients in a large mixing bowl. Separate into individual resealable sandwich bags.

BREAKFAST WRAPS

SERVES 1

1 cup dehydrated
   hash browns
1 cup boiling water
2 flour tortillas

¼ cup shredded
   cheddar cheese or
   cheese powder
2 strips precooked
   bacon

1 small packet ketchup
   or picante sauce
Salt
Ground black pepper

Rehydrate the hash browns by adding boiling water. Set aside for 15 minutes until hydrated, then divide them evenly between the tortillas. Top with the cheese, bacon, and ketchup. Season with salt and pepper to taste. Wrap and eat.

PITA SANDWICH

SERVES 1

1 (2.4-ounce) package
hummus
1 pita flatbread

Sun-dried tomatoes
(optional)
1 (4-ounce) can
sliced olives

$1/2$ cup shredded
Parmesan cheese

Spread the hummus on the pita flatbread and sprinkle with tomatoes (if using), olives, and cheese.

AVOCADO BACON WRAP

SERVES 1 TO 2

1 single-serve packet
mayonnaise
2 flour tortillas

1 ripe avocado, sliced
2 slices precooked
bacon

Salt

Spread the mayonnaise evenly over each tortilla and top with avocado and bacon. Season with salt, roll, and serve.

SWEET MIX

SERVES 4 TO 6

1 cup corn syrup
1/4 cup butter, melted

8 cups Rice Chex cereal

1/2 cup slivered
almonds

Mix the corn syrup and melted butter and heat in a microwave on high for about 1 1/2 minutes. Pour over the cereal and add the almonds. Spread on a cookie sheet and bake at 300°F for 8 to 10 minutes, stirring midway through baking. Let cool, then package in individual resealable sandwich bags.

TOMATO NOODLES

SERVES 1

1 cup dry egg noodles
1 package tomato
   Cup-a-Soup mix
2 cups water

1/4 teaspoon Italian
   seasoning
1/4 cup textured
   vegetable protein,
   beef flavor (optional)

EQUIPMENT
Backpacking stove
Small saucepan

Combine all ingredients in a saucepan and bring to a boil. Reduce the heat and simmer for 10 minutes until cooked.

SPICY ASIAN NOODLES

SERVES 1

1 package ramen
   noodles, any flavor
2 cups water
1/2 cup dried shiitake
   mushrooms
1/2 cup dried corn

2 to 3 cured and
   dried teriyaki beef
   strips (optional)
1 single-serve packet
   soy sauce
Hot pepper sauce

EQUIPMENT
Backpacking stove
Small saucepan

Combine all ingredients except soy and hot pepper sauce and boil for 3 to 6 minutes. Season to taste with the soy sauce and hot sauce.

PIZZA BAGEL

SERVES 1

1 (8-ounce) can
   tomato sauce
1 bagel, sliced

1 tablespoon Italian
   seasoning

1/4 cup Parmesan
   cheese, shredded

Spread the tomato sauce on both sides of the bagel. Sprinkle with the Italian seasoning and cheese. Toast in a skillet over a stove or wrap in foil and place on campfire coals for 5 to 8 minutes.

MASALA CHICKEN AND RICE

SERVES 1 TO 2

1 cup instant white rice
2 cups water
1 package Cream
  of Chicken Cup-
  a-Soup mix
1/2 teaspoon paprika

1/2 teaspoon
  ground cumin
1/2 teaspoon cinnamon
1 (5-ounce) can
  chicken (optional)

EQUIPMENT
Backpacking stove
Small saucepan

Combine all ingredients in a saucepan. Bring to a boil, reduce to a simmer, and cover. Cook until rice is tender and sauce has thickened.

SPLIT PEA SOUP

SERVES 1 TO 2

4 cups water
2 cups dried peas
2 cubes beef bouillon

4 strips precooked
    bacon, cut
    into pieces

EQUIPMENT
Backpacking stove
Small saucepan

At breakfast, bring water to a boil and add the peas. Turn off the heat and cover. Let sit for 6 to 8 hours, until the peas are soft and then return to the heat. Add the bouillon cubes and bacon pieces and cook for 10 minutes.

CHEESY BREAD

SERVES 1 TO 2

1 cup biscuit mix
   (Bisquick)
1 teaspoon sugar
2 tablespoons dry
   powdered milk

¼ cup water
½ cup diced
   cheddar cheese

EQUIPMENT
Backpacking stove
Nonstick skillet

Before the trip, place biscuit mix, sugar, and instant dry milk in a 1-quart resealable freezer bag. To prepare, add the water and cheese to the bag. Zip the bag and knead the dough. Remove dough from bag and stretch it out into 2 rounds, about ¾ inch thick. Place the dough in a nonstick skillet and cook over medium heat for about 6 minutes per side.

PARMESAN AND OLIVE OIL COUSCOUS

SERVES 1 TO 2

2 tablespoons olive oil

2 cloves garlic, diced

1/4 cup shelled pine
   nuts (optional)

3/4 cup plain couscous

1 cup water

1/4 teaspoon salt

1/4 cup grated
   Parmesan cheese

EQUIPMENT

Backpacking stove

Small saucepan

Heat olive oil in a saucepan over medium heat until hot. Add garlic and pine nuts, cooking until garlic is clear and pine nuts are toasted. Add the couscous, water, and salt. Bring to a boil. Remove from the heat. Cover and let sit for 5 minutes. Top with Parmesan cheese and serve.

CARAMEL CHEESECAKE DESSERT

SERVES 2 TO 4

1 small box cheesecake
flavor instant
pudding (substitute
white chocolate
or vanilla)

1 cup dry powdered
milk

1 caramel candy bar,
chopped (Rolo
or Caramello)

3 graham crackers,
chopped

2 cups cold water

Before the trip, combine all ingredients except water in a gallon-size resealable freezer bag. When ready to prepare, add water to the bag and shake and knead to mix. Allow to stand for at least 5 minutes in a cool place before serving.

INDEX

METRIC CONVERSION CHART

VOLUME MEASUREMENTS		WEIGHT MEASUREMENTS		TEMPERATURE CONVERSION	
U.S.	Metric	U.S.	Metric	Fahrenheit	Celsius
1 teaspoon	5 ml	1/2 ounce	15 g	250	120
1 tablespoon	15 ml	1 ounce	30 g	300	150
1/4 cup	60 ml	3 ounces	90 g	325	160
1/3 cup	75 ml	4 ounces	115 g	350	180
1/2 cup	125 ml	8 ounces	225 g	375	190
2/3 cup	150 ml	12 ounces	350 g	400	200
3/4 cup	175 ml	1 pound	450 g	425	220
1 cup	250 ml	2 1/4 pounds	1 kg	450	230

ZAC WILLIAMS has been camping, cooking and taking photos as long as he can remember. He is the author of several cookbooks, including *Spooky Snacks and Treats*. Zac lives in the mountains of Eden, Utah, with his family and numerous pets.